Balance Boldly!

12 strategies to improve relationships, self- care and boundaries!!!

It's Time to Focus!!

SHARON J. LAWRENCE, LCSW-C

Foreword by Vicki T. Sapp, Ph.D.

ISBN: 978-1-7350717-0-1

Design/ Editing: Sharon J. Lawrence, LCSW-C, Rossonio M. Lawrence, BSBM, CPPM

Interior Design: Sharon J. Lawrence, LCSW-C

Dedication

This book is dedicated to every client, friend, family member, mentee, colleague and caregiver who has been trying to manage life better. Here's to you and the new choices you will make in living a more balanced and bold life.

Thank You

Thank you to my AWESOME Husband, Rossonio, for being my biggest supporter and accountability partner when it comes to living life boldly. I am grateful to have my best friend as my accountability partner. I love you, BIGGER!

Thank you to my mentor, Erica Reed, for EVERYTHING! For every check-in, correction, and "Rockstar" reminder. I am grateful for you believing in me!!!

Thank you to my first official mentor and sister-friend, Dr. Vicki T. Sapp! Your never-ending support, encouragement for over 20 years, and investment in my career is appreciated more than you know. Thank you for the contribution of strategy questions to help each reader enhance their experience of living a Balanced and Bold Life. Thank you for teaching me to walk in excellence and to reach for the stars!

Thank you to these special educators and mental health warriors who encouraged me and helped in pulling me out of my comfort zone: Dr. Sharon H. Porter, Dr. Alfiee Breland-Noble & Dr. Anita Phillips. May your work continue to be blessed always!!!

Foreword

My name is Dr. Vicki T. Sapp. I have over 20 years of experience in higher education, 15 of which have been directly focused on inclusion, diversity, equity, access, retention, and success (IDEA+RS). I am an administrator, researcher, educator, and service provider. My research, scholarships and publications, focus on making the inVISIBLE visible.

So, when I was asked to partake in sharing my thoughts about Balance Boldly!, I could not resist. I have known Sharon for over 20 years and during that time, I have witnessed her commitment to serve others in ways to help them grow. Also, she has been instrumental in assisting many of my students and colleagues with understanding the importance of mental health and self-care.

This book is like no other. See, Balance Boldly! is not a book that will allow you to use it as a one and done tool. It is a tool that you will use for a lifetime. Balance Boldly is not a book that is transactional, it is transformative.

Reading this book, will be a staple in your life to use at different stages. It is a journey of examination, exploration, reflection, and action.

As you find the courage to implement the strategies into your daily life, in all areas of your life, I stand in agreement with Sharon that you will truly know how to Balance Boldly!

Balance Boldly is a brilliant masterpiece of 12 Strategies Sharon has put together in one book that she has learned throughout her own personal and professional journey of balancing boldly. You will be equipped, as the reader, with the tools to be empowered to walk in your purpose and to be free… free to walk boldly.

As you read, fully immerse yourself in the journey and the reflection, examination and exploration of your own CHANGE.

Be prepared to pivot and stretch your way of thinking around life and disruptions. You will learn how to love yourself better and fully!!

Get started with reading the book and be sure to write down what resonates with you. Do not wait, get started now!!!

Dr. Vicki T. Sapp

Dr. Vicki T. Sapp, Ph.D.

For more information on Dr. Vicki T. Sapp, please visit www.mentorfirstgen.org

Table of Contents

Introduction

Thank you for stepping up to the plate to finally knock the ball out of the park. I'm sure you are probably thinking you're just going to read another book on inspiration. So, let me set the record straight now! This is not that book!

I need you to approach and read this book with the purpose of allowing action to be a part of your daily functioning.

Every time I have an opportunity to share my heart for a book or one of my journals, the purpose is so readers like you can commit to change.

I know it's not easy when you are confronted with multiple plates in your hands. When you're trying to manage what people consider to be a circus balancing act, it can be very challenging. I can say I have been there. However, I didn't stay there!! Today, I am here to inform you that there are ways of *balancing* your life and doing it *boldly*.

I want you to begin to envision a life with boundaries, structure, and confidence. No guilt, no shame and no apologies. When you're learning to balance things from a bold perspective it means that you are beginning to walk in a level of freedom that is not given to you but that has been created BY YOU, because you are committed to YOU!

Dreams and desires are often impacted and disrupted by many responsibilities and absolutely no boundaries.

Well, that's about to change. Now, for my favorite line.... Let's get started!!!

Strategy 1

Realistic Expectations of Self & Others

"I'm not in this world to live up to your expectations and you're not in this world to live up to mine." – Bruce Lee

Strategy 1: Set Realistic Expectations of Self & Others

Sitting in my office, I plan for an evening that I know is going to be filled with laughter and updates with individuals I cherish. I think of how much time has passed since we have all connected. The anticipation grows and I'm actually nervous about seeing everyone again. I must say that in spite of the nervousness, I push through my feelings and thoughts, and think of the great time I (we) will have. Oh, what a time it will be!

My mind goes over the planned evening. I tell everyone I come in contact with about my plans. Clearly, I'm excited!! It's highlighted in my talk like a huge sign on Broadway. *I'm from the city (NYC), so I actually know what a sign looks like on Broadway. If you don't know, I encourage you to visit the City for the experience of seeing all of the lights. You won't be disappointed.*

Ok, I digress. Let me refocus. As I was explaining, the evening was going to be great!!!! So, I thought.

Fast forward, six hours. I'm sitting in a very important meeting when I feel my phone buzz. I decided to check my phone. What was I thinking?! I know better not to check my phone when I'm in a meeting or about to present. You're probably wondering why. My rationale behind this concept is knowing my mental makeup and my reaction or response to things, it's not the best decision.... at least not for me. Now, back to what happened. I looked at my phone and read a message that made my heart drop... *the evening was CANCELLED.*

Yesssssssss, CANCELLED!!!

I'm sure you can relate. Having something on your list that is important to you and then you find out it's not going to happen. I felt devastated, well not really. That's a little exaggeration. I was actually just very disappointed but, in the moment and in the scheme of things knowing all that I had planned for us made it feel like a devastating moment. The reality is that through all the planning, nothing was so set in stone that I could not adjust to the change. Things happen right? Well on that day, things happened and I had to adjust.

It's ok. In that moment, I was reminded of the importance of being OK when things don't always go my way. I began to think about how we set realistic expectations for ourselves and others. There are going to be moments in life when things are not going to go exactly as planned. Does it mean it's the end of the world?

No! You have to be willing to pivot and to stretch your way of thinking around change and disruptions.

Be willing to learn that change and disruption can be very instrumental in helping you to become more flexible with your thinking. As I think about all of the things we have on our plates and the calendar we use to track every moment, movement and time period even with the most successful strategy, we are still met with things that won't always go our way.

Since we're already talking about us let's proceed with helping us to be a little bit kinder to ourselves. When you are learning to set realistic expectations for yourself, you are learning to be patient and flexible. This simply means that you have to be willing to understand that adjustments in life are necessary. We are not exempt from life or the things that manifest. If you are thinking you are in a fairytale or living the perfect life, I'm sure you've had enough experiences to know it does not feel good when disappointment keeps surfacing. Although many of us still want to believe that the fairytale within our imagination exists, we have to be willing to understand reality is always present. You can imagine and you can pretend to be in a fairytale but the moment you come out of the fairytale you are faced with reality.

Every experience is what teaches us to be more skilled at utilizing our resources to our advantage. When you set realistic expectations for yourself, there should always be a Plan A, a Plan B, and even the ability to adjust "on-the-fly" to the situation.

You should be fully aware of the importance of checking in with others to make sure a plan is still going to take place whether or not it's in your power or theirs. Also, you must be willing to extend grace to others just as if you needed grace extended to you when you're in need of canceling an event or plans.

Maybe I should say that last part again. Many of us seek understanding and grace when we must cancel an event or plans. But for many of us, it is very difficult to extend the same level of grace and understanding to others who are not able to fulfill the commitment they may have made to us. Whether these plans are connected to travel, work or just a self-care day there should always be space that is allowed for life when life happens.

I've learned by extending grace and having it extended to me has taught me the power of balancing things the right way. It means not putting too much pressure on myself or on others to complete tasks. It means I have learned to pivot my movement when necessary.

It also means, it's OK to make mistakes. I've learned not to be so hard on myself and others. When you set realistic expectations, you are not functioning from a fairytale perspective but, you are actually functioning from a real-life perspective allowing you to not only be more patient and kinder but it also allows you to be more at peace.

Setting realistic expectations is all about having a commitment to walk in peace and understanding you cannot control the outcome for every scenario that happens.

Set realistic expectations so you and others. Set your Plan A and your Plan B. If you are feeling a little ambitious set a Plan C. However, remember at the end of the day, none of those plans may work. Be real and honest with yourself about what you can do at any given moment. Be kind and be OK with whatever decision has been made or whatever decision you will have to make. Walk in peace and reality today!

Strategy 1 Reflective Questions:

1. What were the key concepts/ takeaways/ nuggets you obtained from this section?

2. What actions do you take to walk in peace?

Notes:

Notes:

_____

_____

_____

_____

_____

_____

_____

_____

_____

_____

_____

_____

_____

_____

_____

_____

_____

_____

_____

_____

_____

_____

_____

_____

_____

_____

_____

_____

Strategy 2

Increase Understanding of the Needs of Those Around You
(Spouse, Family, Loved Ones)

"Nothing in life is to be feared. It is only to be understood." – Marie Curie

Strategy 2: Increase Understanding of the Needs of Those Around You (Spouse, Family, Loved Ones)

Balancing boldly is about learning what you need to do for you, so you can be better at taking care of you. I know you're wondering about the title of this particular strategy. I want to make sure you understand that in order to take care of others, you have to know how to take care of yourself. In order to take care of others, you also need to understand the needs of those who are around you. Whether you are the caregiver of a loved one, a spouse, a friend, a parent, or child, it doesn't matter because these are relationships that require your attention. They sometimes expect you to move according to whatever their expectations are of you.

Strategy 2 is not about you doing exactly what others expect you to do. It is fully about understanding why people have expectations and what is going on in their lives that may fuel their expectations of you. Sometimes understanding what is happening with others in your life gives you a clear perspective in terms of how to respond.

I think it's important to understand what is happening around you. Often times when setting boundaries, we can function from the perspective of having tunnel vision. Tunnel vision can truly work in your favor when working on a project or trying to get a particular task completed. It has its benefits, but it's also very important not to have tunnel vision if it means others are ignored and disregarded.

In this strategy, I want you to understand the importance of comprehending the needs of those around you, so you can truly respond in a manner that respects them and helps them to understand what is in your control and what is not.

Understanding someone's needs means that you get to respond appropriately and it also helps them to feel like they have not been dismissed. It also shows them how to understand your needs and what is within your control.

I hope you picked up on what I just shared with you.

By having a true understanding of another person's needs and showing them that through the respect you give, it models for them how to also respect the boundaries you have set in place for yourself. So, learning to balance boldly is not just about protecting your peace but it's also about helping people understand that you can respect them while you're on your own journey.

This process is really not that deep but it is necessary in understanding balancing life does not mean dismissing or disregarding others. It simply means that you understand what their needs are while also understanding what your needs are and moving forward in a manner that determines what you can and cannot do at any particular point in time. It is truly about balance and control.

Choose to walk away with a greater understanding and a desire to have patience in learning about yourself and those around you. Increase your understanding of the needs of the people around you as it will make your process easier.

Strategy 2 Reflective Questions:

1. What were the key concepts/ takeaways/ nuggets you obtained from this section?

2. List 3 people close to you and what you believe their needs are?

3. Once you have done that, share how you believe your understanding of their needs models for them how to respect the boundaries you have set in place for yourself?

Notes:

Notes:

Strategy 3

Create New Habits/
Celebrate More

"Good habits are worth being fanatical about."
-John Irving

Strategy 3: Create New Habits/ Celebrate More

One of the biggest challenges I see with people is that they are creatures of habit. It's interesting how I started the sentence about people and then I realized this also includes me. This is also a problem for me! Well, it really depends on what's happening.

You see, one of the things that happens is there are moments in our lives when we start to feel stuck. We try to keep doing the same old things we used to do, causing us to then become very frustrated. One of the biggest challenges is people find it hard to do something new because it may feel uncomfortable. So, we resort to what is familiar.

I don't know about you but when something is happening, I don't want to do something new immediately. I want to do something I've already done in the past, try it again, and hopefully get a different result. Right? Please don't leave me out here by myself as if I am the only one. I know I'm not and I'm sure you have been in this same situation.

What I have learned in my 20 years of being in the field as a social worker and clinician is, we tend to lean in to those things that are familiar and safe. My challenge to my clients, my friends and to myself is to lean in to something different. One of the things we often hear is, "unless you do something different the outcome will always remain the same." Another saying is, "nothing changes, if nothing changes."

There is so much truth to those sayings and quotes. The reality is that there are good and bad habits. Your mission is to create new habits which will produce new outcomes…. change.

In the Power of Habit by Charles Duhigg, Why We Do What We Do in Life and Business, he states, "to modify a habit, you must decide to change it. You must consciously accept the hard work of identifying the cues and rewards that drive the habits' routines, and find alternatives."

Learning how to master this strategy is really about saying, "I need to have courage to try something different so that I can reach a different outcome." It explains the importance to celebrate my small, medium and big wins when I've tried a different approach. This also means even if you don't reach a level of success with the new task, it's imperative to celebrate the fact that you tried something different. Give yourself credit, pat yourself on the back, and say, "go (your name here)!" for doing something different.

It really is OK to create new habits by trying something new. It really is OK to challenge yourself to grow emotionally, spiritually, physically, and intellectually.

How you choose to speak to yourself is going to be critical in moving forward from this moment. As I encourage you to create new habits and to try something different, I am also encouraging you to speak life and to be mindful of how you encourage yourself to do these things and to celebrate taking on something new.

You deserve to have new opportunities but you have to remember not all opportunities come by way of another person. Many of our opportunities come our way because we create them. Walk boldly into your new habit or habits if you are bold enough to do more than one thing at a time. Remember to celebrate. Why? Because you did something new. Enjoy the moment.

We still have many strategies to cover, but I hope and pray you are already encouraged to take on a small task that will put some spice in your day and a pep in your step towards growth and balance. Let's keep going!

Strategy 3 Reflective Questions:

1. What were the key concepts/ takeaways/ nuggets you obtained from this section?

2. What are 3 things you don't have the courage to do, but you want to do?

3. Take each one and apply strategy #1 to make a plan A and B to attempt to accomplish them.

4. Apply Strategy #3 and celebrate the small victories and if you don't succeed celebrate anyway for having the courage to at least try them.

Notes:

Notes:

_____

_____

_____

_____

_____

_____

_____

_____

_____

_____

_____

_____

_____

_____

_____

_____

_____

_____

_____

_____

_____

_____

_____

_____

_____

_____

_____

_____

_____

Strategy 4

Reduce Pressure/
Do Not Create Stress

"Pressure and stress is the common cold of the psyche." -Andrew Denton

Strategy 4: Reduce Pressure/ Do Not Create Stress

According to the Merriam Webster dictionary, *pressure* is defined as, "the burden of physical or mental stress and it is also defined as the constraint of circumstance meaning the weight of social or economic imposition." For the purpose of this section and Strategy 4, I want to initially focus on the first part of the definition which states the burden of physical or mental distress.

When I think about pressure, I think about the expectations we place on ourselves and the demands we set for ourselves to get things done immediately, when they don't have to be. When we function in this manner, we place unnecessary stress and pressure on ourselves which results in mental distress.

When it comes to balancing boldly, it is important to understand how to set things in order and how to do them in a timely fashion. What this means is you learn to identify what needs to be done and how to create a time frame that is realistic.

When there are things you desire to do, don't put pressure on yourself believing it must be done at that very moment. I am not referring to an emergency and the need to respond to something critical requiring your immediate attention. I get it, in those situations you have to react quickly and promptly because it may mean someone's life.

However, if it is not life, limb, or property, SLOW DOWN PARTNER! Assess what is going on. Take inventory and ask yourself what is it that you need to do in order to respond to this appropriately and what tools do you need to make sure you can adequately walk through this situation?

Now, let's look at this second part of the definition when it comes to social and economic imposition. This could mean a lot of things for people who are good with numbers and money and understand how the economy impacts the world. For the sake of this section, I want us to look at how when we place pressure on ourselves, it has the potential to cause us to spend money, time, and emotional investments causing us to spin out of control.

It is imperative when you are looking at the level of pressure and assessing what is happening in your life, that you determine the level of impact in those areas which could possibly destroy relationships or your physical and financial stability.

Understand there will be a ripple effect when decisions are made. Do you want your decisions to be something that creates a positive ripple effect? Do you want to be negative to the extent it impacts areas of your life which includes impact on relationships and your financial stability? You have to decide the level of impact.

When looking at reducing pressure and stress, you must be vigilant in making sure there is a holistic approach to protecting you and what is connected to you. Remember always, you matter and who/what is attached to you matters. Choose life, make better choices, and reduce pressures that don't create positive outcomes.

Strategy 4 Reflective Questions:

1. What were the key concepts/ takeaways/ nuggets you obtained from this section?

2. List 3 stressors currently in your life?

3. What decisions you can make about these 3 stressors that could produce a positive outcome?

Notes:

_____

_____

_____

_____

_____

_____

_____

_____

_____

_____

_____

_____

_____

_____

_____

_____

_____

_____

_____

_____

_____

_____

_____

_____

_____

_____

Notes:

Strategy 5

Set Boundaries

"Boundaries are a part of self-care. They are healthy, normal, and necessary."
– Doreen Virtue

Strategy 5: Set Boundaries

You probably skipped right to this strategy before reading the 1st four strategies. I'm laughing if you did but, if you didn't good for you. In the past two years, I have heard more about boundary setting than I've heard about any of the area related to self-care and emotional wellness.

Although, it is necessary to practice good self-care and maintain good mental health, we are finding people still struggle with the concept and comfort level of creating boundaries to protect their emotional well-being. Individuals also find it very hard to understand that having good boundaries in place potentially impact your mental health.

When setting boundaries, you have to understand your own needs and what works best for you. One of the most common mistakes we can make is having expectations for others that we have not practiced for ourselves. Another mistake made, is that we set boundaries but we're not even sure what it is we're actually protecting. One more mistake... setting boundaries that are fueled by disrespect and disregard for others' feelings.

I'm sure you're stuck with the last statement I made. I know there are individuals out there who will teach us the importance of setting boundaries regardless of what other people may think. There is some truth to that. Your boundaries really are present to protect you but, they are also in place to ensure there is a level of respect that is reciprocated between individuals.

When setting boundaries to help others, set them in a way so others can learn and understand how to treat you and to understand the full path you are currently on.

Unfortunately, there are people who may not care about what it is you're doing for yourself. However, if you have true genuine people in your life who respect you as their friend, family member and colleague they are most likely going to inquire about what's happening with you.

Believe me, this is when you set good boundaries. Individuals get to witness what it is you're doing. It also allows for an opportunity to foster communication between you and others. During this process of communication, it teaches others how you treat yourself in regards to taking good care of you. It also teaches them how to treat you because they understand how much you value yourself.

When setting boundaries please remember it is not about disregarding other people's feelings to the extent that you disregard, dismiss, and destroy the relationship you may have with others. Know this, if the relationship is at the breaking point, most likely there are other underlying issues that were leading up to it. It shouldn't simply be because of how you chose to not communicate effectively in regards to setting good boundaries for you.

I often hear individuals make the comment "I am walking according to my truth." The misconception in this statement is people believe others are supposed to also walk according to their truth. Your truth is simply that, your truth! It doesn't mean others have to walk the same truth. Your communication regarding your shift is meant to help people understand how important your truth and your walk is to you. It is not a guide for them to mirror your walk.

So, coming back to the focus of setting up boundaries. It is not teaching others to do things exactly the way you do things, it is teaching them to respect and understand where you are on your journey.

Remember to understand your "why" in setting boundaries. Is it to ensure that you practice better self-care? Is it to help people understand that you're trying to have a healthy emotional life absent of toxicity? Is it to ensure you prioritize your time with friends and loved ones? Is it so you can improve simple quality care and quiet time for yourself? These are just a few questions to help you understand how to establish a baseline for setting good boundaries. Whatever your focus and mission is regarding how to set your boundaries, make sure you are clear and understand your "why."

Understand when setting boundaries, it should never create more stress internally. It is about having the bandwidth to manage things. Setting good boundaries is about relieving and releasing some of the pressure, stress, and toxicity from your life. This is going to stretch you mentally to think differently and to manage life better.

OK! Let's create realistic boundaries!

Balance Boldly!

Sharon's Steps for Creating Realistic Boundaries

1. Assess your needs. List what you need to remain, improve, and change.
2. Select one thing to work on for the next seven (7) days.
3. Find one person or routine/thing to establish a boundary with.
4. Communicate clearly what you are trying to do for yourself.
5. Schedule a time to commit to that change and maintenance of an action.
6. Be patient with yourself.
7. Be Realistic.
8. Focus on Your Own Needs.

WWW.MYSELAHWELLNESS.COM

Strategy 5 Reflective Questions:

1. What were the key concepts/ takeaways/ nuggets you obtained from this section?

2. List 3 boundaries you have that are deal breakers for you.

3. How do you communicate these 3 boundaries to others to ensure they are respected?

Notes:

Notes:

Strategy 6

Teach Others How to Treat You

"You silently teach others how to treat you by how you treat yourself. Move yourself up your priority list immediately." – Lisa Marie Rosati

Strategy 6: Teach Others How to Treat You

This is a difficult topic for people. Many of us have this mindset that we should treat people as we want to be treated. But guess what? This is not what always happens. If you're anything like me, you've learned that people don't always treat us like they want to be treated and there are moments when we find out that we did not treat people like we want to be treated. Ouch!

You know I'm right! I'm sure you can think back to a time when someone was frustrated with how you treated them. Whether you realized it or it was unintentional, I'm sure you were in shock when you were met with their reaction to your actions.

I don't want you to be shocked any further. I would feel much better if you took the moment to understand the importance of helping others to understand you and you taking the time to understand them.

When attention is given to one's own self it helps you in communicating who you are and what needs you may have. To help you understand where I'm going with this, please take a moment to go with me on this little imaginative trip. Pretend you are scheduling a trip to the spa. In order to plan your spa day or hour, the first thing you think about when you're making the call is what type of massage you would like to receive. You begin to think about all of the things going on in your body, that you need the massage therapist to know about. You also want them to be aware of what areas to focus on. Why? Because you know yourself. You know your body. You know what you need in that very moment and you know what you need them to do in terms of treating you the right way. Your goal is to make sure when you walk out of the spa, that you feel wonderful, catered to and respected.

This is very similar in the relationships you and I have with family members, friends, and colleagues. It's important when communicating with them, that you do so in a way it increases their understanding of your needs. This does not mean they are going to understand you 100% of the time but it is important you make clear what your needs are and your commitment to practicing self-care so others learn to respect it.

What I am relaying to you is, how you communicate your needs and how you treat yourself helps others to know and learn how to treat you appropriately and respectfully.

Have you ever had a conversation with someone about a particular friend's availability? For example, you ask about someone's availability and the person says, "oh, no, Daisy can't help on Tuesdays?" You start to question why. You wonder if Daisy can make changes to her schedule. However, your shared friend insists that Daisy can't because she has a standing commitment to herself and they know Tuesdays are just for Daisy. So, while you are thinking out loud about asking Daisy to make some changes or to make some adjustments, your friend is steadily reminding you that it's a, "no- go" for Daisy.

This is what it should look like when friends look at your actions towards yourself and how they treat you. In order to be respected, people should know you respect yourself and your time.

If there is no self- respect and no regard for the importance of your own life, others will not value you. They will not treat you in the way you want to be treated. When you make a decision not to take care of you in a certain way or in a way that proves you respect who you are, you are truly teaching them to disrespect or disregard you.

However, when you choose to show up and show them you are valuable, important, and loved by you, this is how they learn and know how to treat you. It is imperative you choose YOU first! Not in a selfish manner but to make sure you are well in all aspects of life. When you are well, people who are attached to you get the benefit of feeling the same level of love and respect. It's an overflow if you will. It's a reward. It's an opportunity for them to learn how to treat you and to learn to how to mirror what you do, for themselves should they choose.

Learning to balance boldly is key even in this regard. If you want a balanced life that is full of joy and peace, make sure you're a part of the priorities that you set. This will teach people how to treat you.

Be kind to yourself!

Strategy 6 Reflective Questions:

1. What were the key concepts/ takeaways/ nuggets you obtained from this section?

2. List 3 ways in which you are kind to yourself?

3. How have you seen your 3 ways of kindness to yourself manifest in your relationships with family, friends and love ones?

Notes:

Notes:

Strategy 7

Communicate with Clarity

"Communication- the human connection – is the key to personal and career success."
– Paul J. Meyer

Strategy 7: Communicate with Clarity

Hsjsbshdisnhdvdjwhbdhrhbf. Llllafoajfeo, fonae!
Shsgsjjsh! Jsjshdvjshsbsbnsb-&jddjkshdhs

Hshskjdhjsnbshs

I know you're wondering if this is one of the biggest typos ever or a special code for help! It is definitely not Morse Code or a special code for help. The little jibber jabber you see in the beginning of this section is a clear example of how things can sound or look when you are not communicating with clarity. When there is information missing from your statements or you skip over the most important parts that matter.... communication will be unclear!

The next time you think about the importance of communicating with clarity, I want you to remember the start of this first section with all of those letters that do not create any words or make a complete sentence.

Think about the feeling or thought you had when you first began reading this section. You probably thought to yourself, "OMG! Sharon did not proof read this book at all." Lol! Now, don't get me wrong. I'm sure you may find a word or two that may be misspelled in this book and I pray you will charge it to my head and not my heart.

OK, before I digress too far let me get back to my point. As you can see there is no typo.

Please allow that portion of the section to remain a visual for a moment. Take it with you as a reminder when communicating with others about your needs.

When you are looking at ways to balance it all, the first inclination is to just do what we want without anyone's permission or guidance.

It is clear, you and I do not need another person's permission to do anything. Especially, when it comes to things that help you tend to you. However, if you are attached to people who you may be a caregiver for, a spouse, or a close relative you reside with, you may not be able to fully function in isolation. I know a lot of you who are reading this book are caregivers, married, or even single individuals who still have a lot of responsibilities within their existing relationships. So, this is to guide you in learning how communicating with clarity is not about needing permission, but is simply about helping others to understand you and your movement.

I repeat. Communicating with clarity is not about seeking permission, it is about helping individuals understand what it is you're saying and why you're doing what you're doing. You don't have to go into much detail but you should help them understand you better. Communicating effectively increases understanding. By communicating effectively, it helps others to understand what these 12 strategies in your life are really about.

The Center for Creative Leadership identifies 5 Tips for Effective Communication: "Communicate Relentlessly, Simplify and Be Direct, Listen and Encourage Input, Illustrate Through Stories, and Affirm with Actions."

Something as simple as saying, "Hey Bobby, I'm going to begin making some adjustments to my schedule during the week to prioritize my self-care. I found information on the importance of having a regular self-care routine and I would like to give it a chance. FYI, I will not be available during this particular time so, if you call and I do not answer please leave me a message. I will be sure to get back to you."

This is a perfect example of communicating clearly, and in a simplified and direct manner. There is even a story about finding information on self-care.

Some would inquire as to why someone would need so much information. Giving information, within reason, helps individuals to do the following: hear you describe what you are doing for yourself; helps individuals to create backup plans if they can't reach you during a particular time frame (especially if you are a primary caregiver); helps individuals develop a greater understanding and respect for your time and commitment to self

Communicating with clarity helps others to understand your level of commitment to yourself and consistency with your plan and movement.

Here's the deal, if you are not consistent with the instructions you have given to Bobby or anyone else, you're going to make it very difficult for them to understand that you are making a commitment to yourself. Meaning if you do not respect the importance of what you are doing, how will they?

In addition to the scenario in my description, there are some other things you need to know when communicating with clarity. It's very important to do so with confidence and passion. The passion I'm talking about is not the one associated with people who like yelling. Yikes, not that one. I'm referring to when one communicates in a manner allowing the other person to hear their heart.

The other thing you need to know about communicating with clarity is choosing to connect at a time when you have the other person's undivided attention. You may need to schedule some time with them to talk about what you're trying to do and its importance. You want them to be interested in your plans, your goals, your heart and you want them to understand how important it is to you.

And lastly, when it comes to communicating with clarity, be sure to be consistent and relentless in your message. Don't change what you're trying to describe because they may not see it your way. If they don't agree, it's OK. Respect their opinion but let them know of your plans to continue on your journey or mission. There's nothing wrong with having a discussion but if you know for a fact you are committed to your plan of taking care of yourself and having bold balance, then do so and do it with confidence.

Be confident in the fact that you are choosing a new path of balancing boldly. Do it in a manner allowing the new you to show up, with a new voice and a new determination. Help others to see you grow and change for the better.

Take Good Care of You!

Strategy 7 Reflective Questions:

1. What were the key concepts/ takeaways/ nuggets you obtained from this section?

2. What are 3 things you are confident about that you are able to communicate to others.

3. What do you want to do to allow others to see the new you, with a new voice and new determination?

Notes:

Notes:

Strategy 8

Identify an Accountability Partner

"Accountability is the glue that ties commitment to the result." – Bob Proctor

Strategy 8: Identify an Accountability Partner

What do you think about when you see the words or title, "accountability partner?" When I see accountability partner, I think about someone who is going to hold me to task. I think about the individual who is going to remind me and encourage me of all the things I would like to do. I also think of the individual who is going to push me to reach my goals even when I really do not want to hear or talk about them.

We are really great at coming up with a list of things we want to do and experience during our lifetime. However, we all run into the problem of losing motivation periodically. When we lose motivation, we discover how hard it is to get it back. Well, that is what accountability partners are for. They are the ones who are going to say, "Hey, Rockstar, how's it going with your goals?" At least that is what my mentor, Erica Reed says often!

I can remember about 15 years ago, I had it in my mind to join a sorority. During that time one of my closest and dearest girlfriends, Dr. Vicki, who I affectionately call Brain, etched it in her heart to make sure to encourage me over the years. Brain would give me all things with the colors of the particular sorority. If she traveled, she always brought me back a gift with those colors. Early on, my interest was strong, but not strong enough to pursue. Over time the gifts that she gave me no longer matched my goals however, I grew a wonderful relationship with those colors regardless of my goals changing. I still wear those colors often and people will ask me if I am a part of a sorority and I have to tell them, "nope."

Over time, I realized I no longer had a desire to join a sorority, but other goals surfaced and I pursued them with great passion. In regards to my new goals and plans for myself, I shared with those around me including my girlfriend, Brain, but I realized I did not share with her that I no longer had a desire to join a sorority. I kind of forgot about it.

Well, when I did my most recent Balance Boldly workshop, Brain sent me a text message afterwards which read, "yeah, when are you joining the sorority?" She was letting me know that I was overdue. In that moment, that is when it dawned on me that I never informed her of my change of heart in this area even though she was aware of everything else. I was able to confidently let her know that I no longer had an interest in joining a sorority. She immediately understood and shifted her focus on other goals that I had expressed to her. Even though it was years later, I was honored and grateful to know that she did not forget. This is what an accountability partner will do. They will remember something even when you think you've put it behind you. Even if you don't want to pursue that goal anymore, it is great to know someone is thinking about you and what is important or should I say what was important?

I currently have several accountability partners in my life. Some are for personal goals and others are for professional goals. Either way, those accountability partners have a vested interest in learning about what's in my heart to do and my action plan in reaching those goals. When I'm seeking balance, I'm also seeking a realistic plan of action. My accountability partners are the ones who keep me on task in making sure I take breaks while still making progress.

When I'm setting a timeframe, I make sure to include periods where I may need to pause and reset. In reviewing what it is I am doing, there must always be movement which ensures progress.

My accountability partners are the ones who are not only present to help me keep up with what I set out to do, but they make sure that I am taking care of myself in the process. The mission is not to just reach the goal but it is to make sure that I have a positive experience while moving towards my goal(s) even when I may feel stuck. There's a level of motivation at times and there's a story that comes along with it that eventually helps me on my journey. My experiences turn into testimonies and those testimonies turn into my ability to help others.

Accountability partners teach us how to be accountability partners.

But most importantly accountability partners help you to know that you are not in this alone. When you step into a realm of trying to balance boldly you will begin to experience something you have never experienced before. It is important that you pay attention to every step and feeling as you move forward. Allow your accountability partner to show you things that are beneficial for your journey. Learn to be OK with their strong statements and instructions about how to be successful on your mission.

If you have never had an accountability partner before, please be open to getting one. Start there, start with one! You don't have to be like me with four different accountability partners. Remember, I've been doing this for some time so I've had different goals within different areas of focus over the course of my 20 years in this field. So, by starting with just one accountability partner you will realize that as you learn to step into new things, you may desire to have a different accountability partner for the next journey or keep the one you have if they possess the skillset to guide you on the additional journey. You can have as many as you want or you can have as little as you want, but make sure you have at least ONE.

Be encouraged! Remember to pause when necessary! Do not remain stuck! Remember, balancing boldly is about making sure you're living and balancing your life with boldness.

Strategy 8 Reflective Questions:

1. What were the key concepts/ takeaways/ nuggets you obtained from this section?

2. List 3 accountability partners and how they can hold you accountable?

3. List 3 people you serve as an accountability partner for and how you hold them accountable?

Notes:

Notes:

_____

_____

_____

_____

_____

_____

_____

_____

_____

_____

_____

_____

_____

_____

_____

_____

_____

_____

_____

_____

_____

_____

_____

_____

_____

_____

_____

Strategy 9

Secure a Therapist

"It's only in silence that people can truly hear themselves." – Lori Gottlieb

Strategy 9: Secure a Therapist

One of my favorite books is *Maybe You Should Talk to Someone by Lori Gottlieb: A Therapist, Her Therapist, and Our Lives Revealed.* To make a long story short, this book is about a therapist going to see a therapist. I found laughter and moments of reflection throughout the book confirming what it is like to be a therapist and still not get it right 100% of the time. I am not exempt from life, which means I have to work through things just like you.

The book is also about a therapist and her clients. Lori Gottlieb does an amazing job at ensuring we see the realness and transparency in regards to seeking, receiving and benefiting from therapy. I loved everything about this book. I even reached out to her on Instagram. Guess what? She responded. That made my day. Okay, let's move on.

I am going to make this strategy very, very simple for you. Therapy is for everyone!!! If you've never read my bio, then I should tell you now, that I am a mental health therapist.... also known as the Therapist for Therapists, Professionals, and Couples. No, I am not Lori's therapist. I could only wish, but I must highlight I have some amazing clients.

It's my mission to help individuals make the first step towards therapy with an understanding of how it can address many current/ past issues, ways it can be preventive in efforts to keep matters from worsening and the benefits of committing to having good mental health.

Mental illness is very common among health conditions within the United States. According to the Center for Disease Control (2020), "more than 50% will be diagnosed with a mental illness or disorder at some point in their lifetime; 1 in 5 Americans will experience a mental illness in a given year; and 1 in 25 Americans live with a serious mental illness, such as schizophrenia, bipolar disorder, or major depression."

Trauma and unresolved matters can exacerbate symptoms associated with mental illness. Trauma, mental illness and symptoms can also manifest physically. According to Dr. Bessel van der Kolk, M.D. in his book, The Body Keeps the Score (2014), "overwhelming experiences affect our innermost sensations and our relationship to our physical reality – the core of who we are. We have learned that trauma is not just an event that took place sometime in the past; it is also the imprint left by that experience on mind, brain, and body. The imprint has ongoing consequences for how the human organism manages to survive in the present" (p. 21).

Therefore, when working on things in your life and trying to establish stability, it's important to take care of your emotional well-being. Your mental health must be a priority.

If you are uncertain about how to make this a part of your selfcare plan let me assure you it's not as difficult as it may seem. Finding the right therapist can feel like looking for a job but when you find someone who you're interested in learning more about, you must take the time to ask the right questions and to make sure your questions are answered.

When looking for the right therapist it's important to do the following:

-Inquire about the therapist's professional background and experience in working with your particular symptoms or concerns

-Find out how long they have actually been practicing or at least in the helping profession

-Make sure you find out if they take your insurance or ask about their rates if you do not have insurance

-Ask about their availability and flexibility with scheduling

-Be sure to find out their philosophy about treatment and different treatment modalities utilized in sessions

-If you feel comfortable during your communication with the prospective therapist go ahead and schedule your 1st appointment (in-person or virtually)

Keep in mind, when I say that finding the right therapist is like looking for a job, it really is. If you find after the second or third session that you are not comfortable with your therapist, it is OK to talk to them about your concerns and feelings. Hopefully, your concerns can be addressed fully and you can move forward with your therapy. However, if the matter is not resolved and you do not feel comfortable, notify the therapist that you would like to seek the support of someone else. They will understand.

I can assure you that some therapists are not even aware of there being a problem unless the client informs them. I know it is unfortunate that they would not know, but we do not have a crystal ball or have a magic wand to see what is not said. Your ability to use that moment as an opportunity to talk through your concern(s) may help the therapist in understanding you better. Do not be afraid to express any concerns you may have. Help them to help you better.

The main goal is for you to find a therapist who works for you and with whom you can build a good rapport with, in order to meet your mental health goals.

Please note, it is okay, to not be okay. It is not okay to stay in the "not okay" place. It is also okay to have a therapist, just like it is to have a primary care physician, gynecologist or a cardiologist. It is okay!!

Making the choice to connect with a mental health therapist allows you to talk through your challenges, understand the symptoms you are experiencing, identify realistic goals and objectives which will assist you in working on self and working through difficult moments regardless of your status in life, age, finances, rank or educational background.

Getting help from a therapist who is neutral can be therapeutic and beneficial to your mental health journey. It can be beneficial to every part of your journey!!!

Here are a few resources to help you identify a therapist to help you in this area.

www.psychologytoday.com
www.therapyforpeopleofcolor.com
www.goodtherapy.org
www.therapyforblackgirls.com
www.therapyforblackmen.org
www.traptherapist.com
www.openpathcollective.org

If you are seeking a resource for support groups for individuals with or family members who are impacted by mental illness visit:

www.nami.org (National Alliance for Mental Illness)

Here is a small list of recommended Instagram pages that focus on mental health:

@nianoire
@selfcareforeveryone
@wellseekers
@mentalhealthand_me
@psych_today
@therapyforblackgirls
@good_therapy
@latinxmentalhealth
@thementalhealthmatters

Here is a small list of recommended books:

-Maybe You Should Talk to Someone by Lori Gottlieb

-The Highly Sensitive Person by Elaine N. Aron, Ph.D.

-The Body Keeps the Score by Bessel van der Kolk, M.D.

-The Dumping Ground by Latasha Matthews, LPC

-Staying Sane in an Insane World: A Prescription for Even Better Mental Health by Kiaundra Jackson, LMFT

For a longer list of resources/ recommended podcasts, please visit www.myselahwellness.com/resources

In addition, to these resources you can also connect to a qualified, skilled, and licensed therapists by contacting your insurance company for list of providers in your area who accept your insurance.

Take care of you TODAY!!

Strategy 9 Reflective Questions:

1. What were the key concepts/ takeaways/ nuggets you obtained from this section?

2. List 3 ways in which you can take care of you TODAY!

Notes:

_____

_____

_____

_____

_____

_____

_____

_____

_____

_____

_____

_____

_____

_____

_____

_____

_____

_____

_____

_____

_____

_____

_____

_____

_____

_____

_____

_____

Notes:

Strategy 10

Introduce a Self-Care Plan Into Your Life

"I have come to believe that self-care is not self-indulgent. Caring for myself is an act of survival." – Audre Lorde

Strategy 10: Introduce a Self-Care Plan into Your Life

Once a month I have the privilege and the honor of being a co-host on a local internet show called It's All Business Show for and by Entrepreneurs led by Dr. Sharon H. Porter. On this show, I am affectionately known as the *SelfCarePreneur*. During the show we talk about all things related to business and I get the opportunity to talk about the importance of self-care for entrepreneurs.

It is an enjoyable moment to be able to share the things that work in this area, what research tells us about self-care and the current trends to help entrepreneurs be their best. As a clinician, I am motivated to share tools that either I have learned along my professional career and at times lessons and information received from my mentor, Erica Reed, LCSW-C and other professionals.

Erica is not only one of my mentors but she is also one of my accountability partners and the one I mentioned in Strategy 8. She is serious and means business. She is the real deal and has been very instrumental in my success as a business owner and clinician.

Erica is a Licensed Clinical Social Worker and mental health therapist. She is also a speaker and corporate trainer/ presenter on self-care and workplace health. She has spoken for major corporations and has helped hundreds of business owners become unstuck in the workplace and as leaders.

Erica hosts one of the largest vision board workshops in the DC | Maryland | Virginia area. It lasts for 4 hours and caters to a large group of women who are invested in creating a vision board and establishing goals they can work on over the course of the year.

One of the things I love the most about Erica is that she doesn't just tell you to put things on the paper but she encourages you to attach smart goals to your vision. By having SMART Goals (KazooHR, 2020), it means you focus on goals that are:

Specific- goals are direct, detailed, and meaningful.

Measurable- goals are quantifiable and can be tracked to monitor progress or success.

Achievable- goals are realistic and require tools and resources to achieve them.

Realistic- goals align with your mission.

Time Oriented- goals have a definite time frame and a completion date.

Isn't this great!? Yes, it is. As I write this book, I am able to glance over at my vision board as it sits directly on a shelf next to my desk. The reason the vision board is ever before me is because Erica encourages me and others to be in a constant state of working towards our goals. My mindset is to keep working on my goals as often as possible.

Erica's work is not concluded on the day of the workshop. She continues to connect individually and as a group to ensure that everyone continues to remain motivated. She reviews goals of this amazing cohort of women on a mission to improve their lives.

In order to create and experience results, you must have movement. Many of us have a thought or goal, but we get stuck and find it difficult to gain some traction. Valerie Burton, in her book, Brave Enough to Succeed: 40 Strategies for Getting Unstuck (2014), explains how, "one of the most common misunderstandings that keeps us stuck is the belief that we need to feel inspired to get started. So, we wait for inspiration." She goes on to share how one does not wait for inspiration to move, but by having the understanding to move first, the inspiration will arrive and take root.

What Valerie Burton is saying, is you have to move. How many times have you heard someone or have you heard yourself say, "I do not feel like it or, I do not feel inspired?" Feelings can be a little tricky when it comes to movement.

In 2017, I can remember writing a blog titled, Watch Out for Feelings. In the blog, I highlighted how feelings can really dictate your reality and can cause you to believe that you do not have what it takes to accomplish what you need to do.

In writing this strategy, I had to take my time in helping you to understand the need to have movement and the importance of taking the first step when it comes to practicing good self-care.

Setting goals for a self-care plan is very imperative to your emotional, spiritual and physical well-being. The success of your plan, taps into the best parts of you, allowing you to tap into the best parts of the things around you that you never thought you could experience.

Identify goals that speak to your heart's desire to be the best you. Think in short term time frames (next 30 to 60 days), or think in long term time frames (1 year or longer).

Identify goals connected to your wants and wishes. Let them be things that allow for continuous learning and improvement.

Identify goals that are realistic and will not produce increased stress.

When you set these goals, write them down, post them in a place where you can see them often, and include dates to help you stay committed to a timeline.

Lastly, make sure the goals you create, have small steps to make your process realistic and doable. Be as specific as possible.

Do not wait for the feeling or the inspiration! Just start moving! Introduce a self-care plan today for a better life tomorrow!

Recommended Journal/Planner:

- The Full Focus Planner by Michael Hyatt

- The Bullet Journal

- My Everything Gratitude Journal by Sharon J. Lawrence

Bonus: In addition, to this strategy, I have provided a glimpse of the SC3 Model (3 Steps to Self-Care) that I cover fully during my annual workshop. Enjoy!

SC3 MODEL

1	2	3
SELF-CARE: PRIORITIZE YOU!	SELF-CARE: MINDSET SHIFT!	SELF-CARE: UNDERSTANDING YOUR WORTH!

Sharon J. Lawrence

SC3 MODEL

1
PRIORITIZE YOU!

Schedule Time for YOU!
Be Your Own Friend | Believe in Self
Hobby Anyone!?
Accountability
Stop Apologizing

Sharon J. Lawrence

WWW.MYSELAHWELLNESS.COM

SC3 MODEL

2
MINDSET SHIFT!

Mindset is Everything to Create Habits

The Power of Reframing

Self-Care is NOT selfish | Seek Support

Self-care is Contagious!

Just Do It! #Nike

Sharon J. Lawrence

SC3 MODEL

3
UNDERSTANDING YOUR WORTH!

Know Your Value

Set Limits

Improve Self-Perception

Protect Your Peace

Sharon J. Lawrence

Strategy 10 Reflective Questions:

1. What were the key concepts/ takeaways/ nuggets you obtained from this section?

2. Write down your own SC3 Model (3 Steps to Self-care).

Notes:

_____

_____

_____

_____

_____

_____

_____

_____

_____

_____

_____

_____

_____

_____

_____

_____

_____

_____

_____

_____

_____

_____

_____

_____

_____

_____

_____

_____

_____

Notes:

Strategy 11

Outsource/ Delegate Some Responsibilities

"Few things help an individual more than to place responsibility upon him, and to let him know that you trust him."
– Booker T. Washington

Strategy 11: Outsource/ Delegate Some Responsibilities

As I am writing, the world is facing a global pandemic: COVID-19, also known as the Coronavirus. My advice and recommendations will be a little different than they would have been pre COVID-19.

Prior to this global pandemic my recommendations would have been focused on helping professionals and caregivers connect with the people closest to them whether they are colleagues, family members or friends to get the needed support while weathering the storm of trying to get things done on a day-to-day basis. This recommendation has been altered.

What we find in our past lives or what we consider to be normal behavior or routine prior to this global pandemic has been changed.

I am sure we can all think of a time where we knew we should delegate and ask for assistance but instead we chose to complete whatever the task was on our own. In doing so, the task was met with great frustration and weariness. This is not to blame you or fuss at you for doing more than you should, but it is to highlight past behaviors and the amount of harm it can cause to one's emotional well-being when we don't allow others to help us.

Now, that we have been impacted and continue to face this new reality with COVID-19, we are learning even in the midst of social distancing and quarantining for long periods of time that some are communicating with others more than they would have in the past.

We are finding that some people are more kind, more patient, and that they are more willing to help individuals. What this does is, it allows you to feel more comfortable with not only receiving help from others but it allows you to be more comfortable with having an accountability partner for some things.

In moments like this, you learn to not only ask for help, but you learn to listen when others are offering to help and support. Vulnerability allows you to hear differently and get your needs met.

During this time, more people are working from home and there's been an increase in virtual meetings and phone calls. There is a new fad with virtual lunches, birthday parties, celebrations and check-ins to name a few which allow families and friends to remain connected. This connection can also serve the purpose in helping you to start sharing more of your needs whether they are emotional, financial or physical. Either way you're in a position where you are allowing yourself to be more vulnerable. Being vulnerable or asking for assistance is NOT a weakness. There, I said it!

Vulnerability is Strength Within! Vulnerability is necessary in order to allow yourself to feel more comfortable in having others support you in completing tasks. In order to delegate the responsibility to someone or accept their offer, you have to be willing to allow yourself to let go of some of the control and the mindset that makes you believe you have to do everything on your own.

Although, you may think you are a superhero please remember that the cape does not allow you to fly. Please don't try to fly. It looks cool and it makes you smile, but you cannot fly. What I am saying is you may look the part, but you cannot do it all.

I want to encourage you to think about others in your life and the fact that they are placed in your life for a reason, a season, or a lifetime. Once you recognize what a person's purpose and role is in your life you can then begin to let down the wall and allow them to be what you need them to be.

Delegation of tasks allows others to help you. It also teaches you how to be available to others when they have a need. This type of give and take creates balance. It creates balance within the relationship and your life. When there is balance, there is peace. When there is peace, there is joy.

So, today I encourage you to take a moment and make a list of five (5) people in your life who you can trust to assist you with different tasks. This list can consist of colleagues, friends, and family members who you can rely on. Once you have created the list, start practicing how you are going to start requesting what you need from them. Practice how to be vulnerable. Practice how to listen and respond when they are offering to support. You can do this in the mirror or while you're getting ready in the morning. The goal is that, if you can hear yourself practice, you will become more comfortable when they inquire about your needs. Your practicing now and in the days to come will give you the courage to share with them exactly what you're asking instead of saying, 'I got it." Delegation is help. It is help for you. Please keep that in mind!

Strategy 11 Reflective Questions:

1. What were the key concepts/ takeaways/ nuggets you obtained from this section?

2. What are 3 things you can stop doing and delegate to someone else at home and at work?

Notes:

_____

_____

_____

_____

_____

_____

_____

_____

_____

_____

_____

_____

_____

_____

_____

_____

_____

_____

_____

_____

_____

_____

_____

_____

_____

_____

_____

_____

Notes:

Strategy 12

Listen, Pay Attention, Respond Appropriately

"Yet they did not listen or pay attention; they were stiff-necked and would not listen or respond to discipline." – Jeremiah 17:23

Strategy 12: Listen, Pay Attention, Respond Appropriately

One of the biggest challenges I see with individuals is the inability to listen carefully to what is being communicated. When I ask individuals to describe their communication style, they respond with, "I'm a good communicator, I am able to say what I think and feel." I can guarantee you that when this is said, most individuals really believe that until I inquire more about their understanding of communication, in particularly effective communication.

I use the moment as an opportunity to help them understand what it really means to communicate and what happens between two or more individuals during a communication exchange.

Not everyone knows how to communicate, meaning not everyone knows how to express themselves in a manner where the other person can receive what is being communicated. It also means that not everyone knows how to listen carefully to what is being shared with them. This tells me that not everyone has learned the art of managing their listening and speaking skills.

According to Kim Krisco in Leadership & The Art of Conversation (2004), "the notion of managing your listening may seem even more strange than managing your speaking, but mastering the art of listening will transform not only your conversations but your life." He describes how we are often on automatic and as a result, I see the potential for mental car accidents because we do not pay attention to how the voice inside impacts our ability to listen well. Therefore, our reactions can create conflict.

My work is helping individuals understand the power of communication when done right. It is okay to say what you think and feel, but it is equally important to deliver it in a way the communication can be received.

I often describe communication like a carefully wrapped package. The goal is for your communication (or gift) to be received in the way in which you intended...with care and clarity. There's understanding and grace that accompanies it, allowing for ongoing communication.

Think about it. When someone is communicating with you, are you listening to understand or are you listening to respond? Hopefully, you're listening to understand which means you are receiving the message and listening to the words that are coming out of their mouth and you are taking in the information with intentionality. Intentionality means you are intentional about listening and making sure you heard not just the words but the person's heart. When one fully listens to what is being said and pays attention, this allows for a proper response.

A proper response means you are able to respond completely, thoroughly, and appropriately to what has been shared.

This removes the desire to respond in defense or change the topic to prove a point. When it comes to balancing things, you are taking a moment to improve the way you communicate with others.

I know that I took the long way in explaining this and you are trying to understand what this has to do with ways to Balance Boldly. When it comes to balancing things boldly, I need you to truly understand that you are taking every moment in your life seriously including the way you communicate with others.

Since communication is a two- way street meaning it is reciprocal, you will need it to understand who you are connected to and their needs. You will also need effective communication to help them in understanding you and your needs.

As family members, professionals, caregivers, colleagues, whatever your title may be, we have a lot on our plates. We may be great at communicating what it is we do for work and for others, but we lack skills in communicating around matters that speak to our personal journey and our needs.

I love how Krisco (2004), breaks down the difference between *"reactive listening and proactive listening."* Reactive is "listening to," while Proactive is, "listening for." This is something I teach in my work with therapy and anger management clients.

Basically, you are either listening to react with a quick defensive statement because you missed what was being said, or you are listening for an opportunity to understand and appropriately respond to the other person.

Remember, communication is reciprocal. Whether you are the deliverer or the receiver be mindful of how you choose to respond. Will it be REACTIVE or PROACTIVE?

Let your thought process be to listen to understand so you can communicate well. Be OK with seeking clarification when you are unsure about what is being said. Your goal in communicating well is to make sure you are not carrying any negative energy that does not serve you or the other person well.

Your goal is to communicate in a way that creates and maintain peace.

Communicating well allows for healthy relationships to be established and to be maintained.

Protect your mind, protect your heart, and protect your relationships. If you find that others are not communicating well, encourage them to take a pause from the discussion until you both can come back and communicate more effectively.

Let them know what you both have to share is very important to you. In doing this, you teach them how effective communication can exist in relationships.

Choose to communicate in a way to save your relationships.

Choose to communicate in a way that helps you live a more peaceful and balanced life.

Choose a better way to communicate today.

Strategy 12 Reflective Questions:

1.   What were the key concepts/ takeaways/ nuggets you obtained from this section?

2.   List 3 people you could communicate with differently in effort to save your relationship with them?

Notes:

_____

_____

_____

_____

_____

_____

_____

_____

_____

_____

_____

_____

_____

_____

_____

_____

_____

_____

_____

_____

_____

_____

_____

_____

_____

_____

_____

Notes:

Next Step: The Application

"Knowledge has no value except that which can be gained from its application toward some worthy end." – Napoleon Hill

The Application:

According to Merriam-Webster Dictionary, Application means, "an act of applying; an acting of putting something to use, an act of administering or laying one thing on another, and attention."

Now, that you have successfully made it through reading the 12 strategies of learning to balance boldly this is the moment where we discuss the process of application.

In order to apply something, it means you have to follow the instructions to carry out an act. In regards to the 12 strategies to balance boldly, you must apply the knowledge so that you can do something and obtain different results.

It is my hope that by this point you are feeling more devoted to having a more balanced life. This means that you are in a position to have a better relationship with yourself as well as others. It also means you are taking steps to live a life that is filled with more peace of mind.

In no way am I telling you that life is going to be perfect because it's not. What I am saying to you is, the life that you are choosing to live now is because you are rewriting the narrative. You are in control of how you manage each moment of your day and the rest of the days of your life.

This is a moment of change. I am calling you to make a shift and I am calling on you to recommit yourself to a life that is truly worth living. Regardless of how you feel, it is not about feelings. It is about your commitment to move forward. You deserve it. You deserve to live well emotionally, spiritually, and physically.

So, let's commit to this change today.

Read this statement aloud:

I, _____, will no longer be bound by the past or the unrealistic expectations of self and others. Today, I choose to take the first step to a better life.... a bold and balanced life. I recommit to myself today! I will dream again! I will exercise self- care! I will be patient with myself! I will set healthy boundaries! I will continue to help others without destroying myself in the process! I will do Better! I will not shrink back to the old ways of thinking and living!! I will be NEW NOW! I Will Balance Boldly!!! (Now Clap Loudly for Yourself!)

Congratulations!!! You are New and Bold! I am proud of you for making this recommitment to yourself and for being ready to apply this knowledge that will change your life for the better. Let's walk boldly together!

Next Steps Reflective Questions:

1.   What are you able to control in your life?

2.   What is your new narrative?

Notes:

Notes:

_____

_____

_____

_____

_____

_____

_____

_____

_____

_____

_____

_____

_____

_____

_____

_____

_____

_____

_____

_____

_____

_____

_____

_____

_____

_____

_____

Notes:

Notes:

Epilogue

Thank you so much for taking this journey with me. I truly hope that you were able to glean some amazing strategies and steps to help you on your journey to living a more balanced and bold life.

Writing during a time when COVID-19 continues to impact the world, I realize this is the perfect time to share this book with the world. We were facing many things before this pandemic and things have exacerbated the impact of trying to juggle it all.

Even in the midst of these changes, it is truly my hope and desire that these 12 strategies and the application process will help you in doing something different. I encourage you to take the first step in recommitting to yourself so that you can be a better you, a better friend, a better family member, and/ or a better caregiver!

Selah,

Sharon

References

Application. (2020). In Merriam-Webster Online Dictionary. Retrieved May 2, 2020, from http://www.merriam-webster.com/dictionary/application

Burton, V. (2014). Brave Enough to Succeed. (pp. 137-138). Harvest House Publishers. (Originally published as Get Unstuck, Be Unstoppable).

Centers for Disease Control and Prevention, (2018 January 26). Learn About Mental Health- Mental Health- CDC, Retrieved April 28, 2020 from https://www.cdc.gov/mentalhealth/learn/index.htm

Duhigg, C. (2014). The Power of Habit. Why We Do What We Do In Life and Business. (pp. 270). Random House, LLC. (Original work published 2012).

Gottlieb, L. (2019). Maybe You Should Talk to Someone. A Therapist, Her Therapist, and Our Lives Revealed. Boston | New York: Houghton Mifflin Harcourt

Krisco, K.H. (2004). Leadership & The Art of Conversation. *Conversation As A Management Tool.* (pp. 76-80). Mumbai. Jaico Publishing House. (Original work published in 2002).

Pressure. (2020). In Merriam-Webster Online Dictionary. Retrieved April 1, 2020, from http://www.merriam-webster.com/dictionary/pressure

Sapp, V.T. (2020). Strategy Questions for Balance Boldly.

Van der Kolk, B. (2014). The Body Keeps the Score, Brain, Mind, and Body in the Healing of Trauma. (p. 21). New York, NY: Penguin Books.

What is a SMART Goal? Kazoo. (2020). Retrieved May 2, 2020 from Https://www.kazoohr.com/resources/library/how-to-set-smart-goals

5 Tips for Effective Communication, Center for Creative Leadership www.ccl.org retrieved 4/27/2020.

About the Author:

Sharon J. Lawrence,

LCSW-C, LCSW, ACSW, EAS-C, CAMS-II, BC-TMH

Therapist | Speaker | Author | Consultant

Mrs. Lawrence is a Therapist for Therapists, Professionals and Couples. Her passion is to improve the lives of clinicians and professionals who manage the day to day responsibility of caring for others. It has been proven that this type of care can produce secondary trauma in addition to discovering and revealing past trauma and mental health challenges.

Mrs. Lawrence is committed to helping couples strengthen and revive their relationships through counseling using the Prepare/Enrich® assessment and curriculum. She provides both short and long-term counseling through the use of Cognitive Behavioral Therapy, Solution Focused Therapy, Motivational Interviewing, and Eye Movement Desensitization Reprocessing (EMDR).

Mrs. Lawrence is a Licensed Clinical Social Worker (LCSW-C/ LCSW), Certified Anger Management Specialists-II (CAMS-II), Certified Prepare-Enrich Facilitator and Trainer, Certified

Life Coach, Board Certified-TeleMental Health Provider (BC-TMH), an Approved Clinical Supervisor in Social Work (MD) and credentialed as an Employee Assistance Specialist-Clinician. She also holds a Certificate in Christian Ministries from the Evangel Bible College in Upper Marlboro, MD. She has 20 years of experience working with children, adults, couples and families within the following settings: mental health, substance abuse, foster care, family court, and developmental disabilities.

Mrs. Lawrence is the co-host of It's All Business Entrepreneurship (Special Segment of The I Am Dr. Sharon Show) on Urban Style Media every 3rd Sunday from 10:00- 11:00 am. She is affectionately known as the SelfCarePreneur where she provides information on mental health, self-care, and trends related to emotional well-being aspect for business owners. She has been a subject matter expert on Good Morning Washington, Radio One's Winston Chaney Morning Show, Let's Talk Live, BMore Lifestyle, Prepare/Enrich®, and a number of conferences to include Boris L. Henson Foundation Can We Talk? Mental Health Conference. Mrs. Lawrence has also been featured in media publications and podcasts such as but not limited to Yahoo! Lifestyle, Bustle, The Root, Madamnoire,

GoodTherapy, ArlNow, OldPodcast, I Am CEO Podcast, The Incubator Podcast, and Worth to Wealth Podcast. In addition, Mrs. Lawrence is an Adjunct Professor for Bowie State University (Department of Behavioral Sciences and Human Services) and Prince George's Community College (Department of Human Services) where she is helping to prepare the next generation of helping professionals.

Other Books by the Author:

7 SIMPLE WAYS TO SHAPE YOUR MARRIAGE: STRATEGIES TO FEELING LOVED AND CONNECTED

Sharon offers couples simple ways to reboot their thinking around marriage and how to improve their relationships with being intentional. Each area of this book provides information on how important it is to work together with a stronger commitment to one another.

MY EVERYTHING GRATITUDE JOURNAL: 31- DAY GRATITUDE JOURNAL FOR SELF-CARE AND EMPOWERMENT WITH BONUS GOAL SETTING GUIDE

This is where gratitude meets journaling. With this journal, you will discover a powerful tool to not only improve one's mood, but also your perspective on EVERYTHING that impacts your life.

Color: PEACH (For Adults)

MY EVERYTHING GRATITUDE JOURNAL: 31- DAY GRATITUDE JOURNAL FOR SELF-CARE AND EMPOWERMENT WITH BONUS GOAL SETTING GUIDE

This is where gratitude meets journaling. With this journal, you will discover a powerful tool to not only improve one's mood, but also your perspective on EVERYTHING that impacts your life.

Color: BLUE (For Adults)

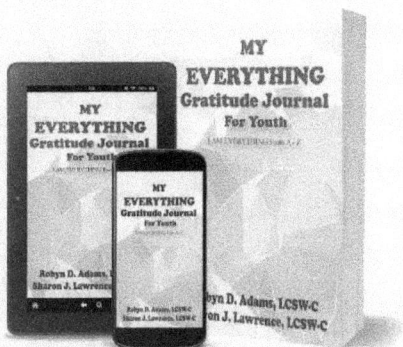

MY EVERYTHING GRATITUDE JOURNAL FOR YOUTH: I AM EVERYTHING FROM A TO Z

Co-Author: Robyn Adams, LCSW-C

Where the young mind develops gratefulness while journaling. For every young person, there is a period in their life where they must learn to express themselves, see themselves, and develop gratitude about who they are from A to Z. There is something powerful in knowing early on how important you are to everyone around you. This journal is the perfect tool to help them find and protect their purpose.

To purchase please visit:

www.myselahwellness.com/shop

(*for signed copies*)

or

www.amazon.com/author/sharonjlawrence

To Book Sharon please visit:

www.myselahwellness.com/booksharon

or

email booking@myselahwellness.com

Sharon would love to hear from you. If you would be so kind, please visit her Amazon page and leave a review so that others may know how you felt about the book.

www.amazon.com/author/sharonjlawrence

Looking forward to seeing you at the next Balance Boldly workshop in January.

www.ingramcontent.com/pod-product-compliance
Lightning Source LLC
Chambersburg PA
CBHW020910090426
42736CB00008B/570